D0835849

Tips From Widows

Tips From Widows

Jan Robinson

BLOOMSBURY

LONDON · NEW DELHI · NEW YORK · SYDNEY

First published in Great Britain in 2013

This edition first published in 2015

Bloomsbury Publishing Plc
50 Bedford Square
London
WC1B 3DP

www.bloomsbury.com

Bloomsbury is a trademark of Bloomsbury Publishing Plc

Bloomsbury Publishing, London, New Delhi, New York and Sydney

A CIP catalogue record for this book is available from the British Library

ISBN 978 1 4088 6553 8

10 9 8 7 6 5 4 3 2 1

Typeset by Newgen Knowledge Works (P) Ltd., Chennai, India
Printed and bound in Great Britain by CPI Group (UK) Ltd, Croydon CR0 4YY

In memory of my husband, Tony

Contents

Foreword

This is a wonderful, beautiful little book.

It is like a quiet wise friend, full of comfort and practical counsel, when your world has collapsed or changed beyond recognition.

It is like a crib sheet of how to cope; it is as helpful to friends of widows as to the widows themselves, and it is written from experience, which is the bedrock of reliable advice.

Joanna Lumley

Preface

This book makes no claim to be an authority on how to cope as a widow, nor does it set out to offer a thorough analysis of widowhood. It is, quite simply, tips from widows. No book can cover the needs of widows of any age. Grief is an unmanageable emotion and the form it takes is unique to every woman whose husband or partner has died.

Three weeks before my husband died suddenly and quite unexpectedly, I had answered an invitation to a lunch party being held for a widow who was marrying again at the age of seventy. When the time came I dilly-dallied as to whether I could cope with going. I took courage and went. I knew only a few of the fifteen women (not all of whom were widows) there, and after a few minutes seated next to a woman I had not met before, she told me that she had been a widow for five years. I said, 'I've never been a widow before. Please give me a few tips.' She did. That is how this book started. At the back of this little volume I have listed the names of all the widows who have contributed their thoughts. Most of them are over fifty years old.

I hope that some of these tips will encourage a smile or a nod of understanding. You are not alone. It is tempting to say that there are no dos and don'ts. However, this is not entirely the case, because there do seem to be a small number of things that the vast majority of widows will agree should or should not be done. This said, the rest really is a matter of opinion; points of view that you might or might not accept.

As my husband once said, 'Advice is for listening to, but not necessarily for taking.'

Being a widow is not an illness; you can't take a pill and make it all better. You can only cope as best you can, and we all do it differently. There are no set rules about coping with loss. Some people struggle with it for years and maybe never get over it. Others manage to move on. You are alone in your boat on the ocean, but I hope that this book will help you to recognise that other boats are out there too.

Unfortunately, some of the tips in this book – the financial ones especially – will also be of use to women who know or sense that widowhood is imminent.
In other words, if your husband is about to die, there are some things that it is essential to do before he goes. You will find this information towards the end of this book.

That, briefly, is what this book is. It seems sensible, also, to add a few words about what it is not.

It is not intended for young widows (say, below the age of fifty); by the same token, it is not intended for widows with small children; nor is it primarily for widowers, since many of the problems faced by widowers are quite different from those faced by widows.

It is, quite simply, tips from widows of a certain age whose families – if they have them – have grown up and left home; and it is aimed, on the whole, at other widows in a broadly similar situation.

At the end of this book there are a few spare pages. These pages are for you to add any further tips and useful sayings.

A last thought. The definition in the Oxford English Dictionary of the word 'widow' is: 'A woman who has lost her husband by death.' For many people, this conjures up a certain image of a figure who is wearing black, lonely, sad and vulnerable. Would your view of a black widow spider be different if it were called an orange widow spider? Let me suggest another way of looking at the word 'widow'. Thus:

Wise · **I**ntegrated · **D**ignified · **O**ptimistic · **W**oman

Part I

Before he dies

Money I

A widow wrote to say that she had to really encourage her husband, when he was ill and later near death, to talk to her about all the practical implications that would occur after he died. Many men are reluctant to do this.

> **Tip 1** Encourage each other to talk about these matters well before either person has become too ill.

It is essential to have a joint account with your husband. (For more details, see the Appendix, page 65.)

The moment your husband dies, any bank account in his sole name will immediately and automatically be frozen, even if you are the sole beneficiary of his will. So if, say, your husband was responsible for all money matters, and if he ran everything from an account in his name only, you will be unable to access any money at all.

This is what happens by law. Specifically, any account in his sole name will remain frozen from the moment he dies until probate is complete; and this process often lasts up to six months, and can last even longer. Note, too, that all Direct Debit payments that have been set up for this account will also stop immediately; so that if all Direct Debits for your household go through an account solely in the name of your husband, your entire life will quite literally come to a halt.

A first example. The son of a wealthy couple had to spend over a year sorting out the intricacies of the tax situation left by his two elderly parents, and had to spend £60,000 of his own money to cover the cost (professional fees, etc.) of this process (as I say, the son's parents were very comfortably off). When, finally, probate was complete, he got his money back. But what if he hadn't been able to find it in the first place?

A second example. An elderly widow knew that she was going to die imminently, and therefore gave her daughter a cheque for £15,000 to cover the expenses that would inevitably be incurred in the aftermath of her death. 'Put it into your account now,' she said to her daughter, 'and make sure it is cleared before I die.' The bank cleared it eight hours before she died; if they hadn't, it would have been worthless.

Tip 2 It is absolutely essential to do one of the following two things.

Set up a joint account with your husband, and make sure that all Direct Debit payments for your family and household go through this account (and not through a sole account in your husband's name).

Set aside a sum that you know will be sufficient to carry you through the worse-case probate scenario.

One last and very important tip is regarding pensions. To put it bluntly, if you and your man have simply been co-habiting for a long time, after his death you will not be regarded as his legal widow. You will be unable to receive any widow's state pension. However, your partner will very probably be able to nominate who should benefit from his professional pension after his death.

Tip 3 Only if it is what you both wish, get married or become civil partners! Do so at once or at least make the appropriate pension nomination if that is what you both want.

Part II

When he dies

Funeral director

All the information and help you need will be provided by the funeral director just after the death of your husband, and he will guide you through everything you need to know. If you know your husband is dying, do choose a funeral director who you feel is sympathetic to the requirements of both spouses. In the event of your husband's sudden death, this will, of course, not be possible.

It is so easy, with the emotional turmoil, to forget to tell the funeral directors to let you know, after the cremation, when the casket will be available to be collected.

Registrar

Registering the death of your husband can be a very painful experience, so take along a friend or relative, since with your emotions awry, you will probably not be able to concentrate. You will be given printed material, including information about immediate cancellations that are required for your new status. A widow said that she found her registrar gentle and understanding. You don't have to remember much of what the registrar says, because he or she will talk you through it. It is a legal process that has to be done, and you should be aware that it will be upsetting.

The registrar will as a matter of course give you a death certificate, and will also ask you whether you would like further copies, which will be official documents, and not standard photocopies. Do be sure to take this opportunity to ask for at least half-a-dozen copies of this vital document. A whole range of professionals will require it, and photocopies won't do. The document, I repeat, must be generated by the registrar.

Tip Take a friend.

Funeral

Some religions traditionally lay down that the funeral should take place immediately after death. Others, on the other hand, allow more time. In this case, whether you have a church service or a service at a crematorium, or both, you can therefore think about the way you wish things to be done.

Sometimes, after the death of your husband, a post-mortem may be required by law. This can delay the burial or cremation, and you will have to wait until the body is released to the funeral directors. This can be most upsetting, but there is no getting round it.

Tip 1 Do involve your children in all the arrangements and decisions with regard to the funeral arrangements for their father; also, take your time, if you follow a religion that allows that.

Tip 2 Do encourage grandchildren to go to the funeral or cremation. In the case of very young children, it is for the parents to decide whether they should attend.

Tip 3 In the very early days following your husband's death, the telephone will ring constantly. The emotional strain of answering every call will often be too great. It is therefore a good idea to switch on your answerphone whenever you feel like it, or alternatively, to get a friend or adult child to answer on your behalf.

Dressing for mourning

Some widows feel that it is appropriate to dress in black – or at any rate in subdued colours – for a certain period following the husband's death. Some opt for bright colours. Others feel no need at all to change the way they dress. The choice is entirely yours.

Letter writing

You may or may not receive letters, cards, or even emails of condolence. One widow I know received several hundred letters, and was also surprised to receive a number of emails, which at the time struck her as being rather informal, although they were also comforting; especially since the emails arrived straight away, whereas the letters came in more slowly.

As for the way to reply to these messages, it is really up to you. You might wish to reply to emails with emails, to letters with letters. The choice is yours. You will, however, almost certainly find it impossible to write long letters to everyone who contacts you, and some widows find it convenient to send out standard cards. There also has to be a cut-off point for replying, and several people have suggested to me that this should be three months after the death of your husband.

> **Tip** In the end, the choice as to whether to reply, and when, is entirely yours.

Afterlife

There are many different views – some religious, others not – about what will happen to your husband after he dies. Does he exist in some form? Can he hear me? Or does he perhaps not exist in any form at all? Your perception or your belief is your own truth. You may change your views, but do not let anyone else tell you what to believe. Some widows have told me that they walk round their home talking to their dead husband in the belief that he can hear them.

You might consider keeping your husband's ashes to put in your own coffin one day. However, keeping the casket on show in your home sometimes creates problems with family and visitors, so discretion might be a good idea.

Accountants

If you have an accountant, do not change firms during the first year of widowhood.

If you do, it might appear to the Inland Revenue as an indication that you are perhaps trying to avoid paying the full tax you owe.

For example, a recently widowed woman aged 63 was asked by the Inland Revenue to produce a record of all monies received and paid by her and her husband over the previous seven years. The Inland Revenue had no reason to suspect any wrongdoing at all; nevertheless they are fully within their rights to review all accounts, without providing any reason, going back over seven years. Therefore, even though neither the widow nor her recently deceased husband had done anything untoward, and even though their joint accounts were in perfect order, she had to pay her accountant £7,000 to do the job, which involved weeks of painstaking work.

Tip For seven years after you are widowed, take out professional fee protection (your accountant can deal with the practicalities) to cover the risk of this happening to you. Approximate annual cost: £80 ... which is money well spent, considering the possible downside.

If you doubt the wisdom of this tip, bear in mind two things. Firstly, it comes from an experienced accountant who has seen it happen before. Secondly, and more generally, you should be aware that since the country's finances are in a state of some disorder (to say the least!), the taxman is more hungry for your money than ever before.

Another story in a similar vein. At her husband's funeral, a widow was approached by another mourner who said he had been a colleague of her deceased husband. He offered to help her with her financial affairs, and without thinking straight, she accepted. He lost her a great deal of money, and worse besides.

Several widows have told me that they found it useful to take a small tape recorder along to meetings with the accountant, so as to be able to play back the more complicated parts of their meetings and understand them at leisure. Especially in the immediate aftermath of a husband's death, many widows – however intelligent – are not in a state of mind to absorb even quite basic financial instructions. (For more details on accountancy matters, see the Appendix, page 65.)

Part III

The months after
he dies

Other people's reactions

There have probably been times in all of our lives when we have not been able to fully comprehend or empathise with a recently widowed woman. Some people cannot find the right words and seem unable to face you. Others may not mention your husband's name, or might not speak to you at all; and others might even cross the road in order to avoid bumping into you. All this is very painful, but the truth is that we never really know what is going on in other people's minds.

For this reason, it is best not to get offended by the comments that you will hear. For example:

'Now you're back on the market again.' (Married man to widow six weeks after her husband's death.)

'I know just how you feel. My dog died yesterday.'

A friend to a recently widowed woman on taking leave of her: 'Bye, Sarah. I won't be seeing Peter [the deceased husband] in a rush, will I?'

'Granny, are you now a weirdo?'

'This is fucking awful for you. When you feel stronger, we'll go and watch penguins somersault.'

Four days after the death of her husband, a grandchild said to the widow: 'Granny, will you be marrying again?'

An older widow approached a recently widowed woman who was at the hairdresser's having her hair done on the morning of her husband's memorial service. 'I'm so sorry to hear about your husband,' said the older woman, 'and I just wanted to tell you: it gets worse.'

Almost invariably, these comments and many others like them – often quite astoundingly inappropriate – are not the result of conscious thought at all. People will often say the first words that come into their minds, however foolish or even offensive.

Tip Do not be offended. They don't mean it.

Also, try not to feel hurt when you are left out of some people's lives. Suddenly, some couples you know don't contact you any more. Fitting in a single woman socially might not be easy for them, and you have to realise that you have now joined the band of single women. It will happen. Furthermore, your own company is worth enjoying, and the new space in your life that comes with widowhood is some sort of compensation.

Children

It is easy to become too self-absorbed in your own grief and if you have adult children they too will be feeling the huge loss of their father and will also be very concerned about you. Although you will be able to share some of your grief with them, it is sometimes difficult. As one widow remarked, she always falls instantly into the role of mother and wants only to comfort them. She said it was a very strange and upsetting time for all of them, as their personal reactions were all so different. One adult son coped with his loss by writing a book about his father, including old family photographs. He had it printed for his mother and his siblings. Her other children talked of their father the whole time, or hardly at all. She said she took comfort when telling her children, 'Remember, your father will always be with you and in you; half your genes are his.'

Another widow said that with the passing of time, she could increasingly see the physical and behavioural characteristics of her husband in her own children, which was often painful and comforting at the same time.

Another widow said that one of the compensations of her heart-rendering loss was to see her husband replicated in many small ways in her grandchildren. She found this a great solace.

Grandchildren

They, too, need to be comforted and to be able to talk freely about their grandfather. Allow them to comfort you as well. Encourage them, even if it brings tears to all of you. Their perception of their grandather will be quite different from their parents' perception of him, and will be a bonus for all the family.

> **Tip** Talk.

Crying

Tears are a unique liquid that your body produces. There's nothing like it. They bathe the soul. You will cry on and off, for the rest of your life, and the tears will often be triggered by the smallest thing, generally a happy or beautiful memory that might come to you at any time.

Listening to music is a blessing that can bring memories of joy or sadness. A widow said she often, when driving on the motorway, listens to the radio. A piece of music might suddenly bring an instant blurring of tears. She advises to turn the radio off immediately, even if the temptation is to continue to listen. You will need all your concentration and sight!

One widow gave an analogy. She said she felt like an old rubber hose pipe that had been left lying in the garden for many years, which, when trodden on by mistake, unexpectedly squirted out a huge gush of water.

However, just occasionally the tears will not come. One widow found herself unable to cry. The sudden shock of losing her husband was so intense that she sought the help of a professional therapist.

Tip Don't be surprised to find yourself crying, even after many years.

Flashbacks

It is normal – certainly for a number of months after your husband's death – to have flashbacks to images of him lying dead. These can be very vivid and real, and are always deeply upsetting. If these flashbacks continue for any length of time, you should seek help.

Absentmindedness

One widow told me the following amusing story – admittedly many, many years ago.

Shortly after her husband died, she flew to the USA and before she landed was given an immigration form to fill out. Without thinking, she went down the list ticking all the 'yes' boxes, not the 'no' boxes. So to the questions 'Are you carrying a gun?' 'Do you have any drugs on your person?' 'Have you ever been sent to prison?' 'Are you a communist?' 'Do you intend to overthrow the US government?' ... to all these questions, she absentmindedly answered 'yes'. Unfortunately the US immigration authorities failed to see the funny side of it, and she was detained for a considerable time.

> **Tip** You will inevitably do some foolish things.

Alcohol and pills

Some widows will be tempted to drown their sorrows in alcohol, or to seek oblivion with antidepressants.

Besieged as we are by bossy government health warnings, we all know that alchohol is a depressant, and it stands to reason that the last thing a widow wants or needs is to be more depressed than she already is. In other words, alcohol is not the ideal long-term solution to the many problems of widowhood.

That said, we all know what pleasure a few glasses of wine bring. The trick is getting the balance right.

One widow I heard of, who had always drunk moderately and socially, started to drown her sorrows shortly after her husband died. From lunchtime onwards she would almost invariably have a glass of white in her hand, and by the end of the evening she would be more or less blotto – slurring her words, unsteady on her feet (particularly on the stairs), maudlin. Among the many worries that this engendered in family was the fear that she would nip out in the car and cause serious damage to herself and others. Unfortunately no end to this story is in sight.

For depression and sleeplessness, pills are sometimes very helpful, but for limited periods only. For example, two widows said they wished they had gone to their doctor earlier to ask for help – one for depression and the other for sleeplessness – in the initial painful first year. They later concluded that they had tried to be too brave. One of them said that the combination of mourning and sleeplessness had been a nightmare.

The shock of losing your husband can sometimes bring on hyper-anxiety in some widows. Talk to your doctor. This shock can deplete the natural seratonin in your body. This can be built up again by temporarily taking medicine for this condition.

Alternatively, if you believe in homeopathy, seek help from your practitioner. Both allopathic and homeopathic treatments can help.

Contrary tip (from an elderly widow) :
'Have plenty of wine and just let emotions happen.'

Psychological higher education

After the death of your husband your brain will not always be in gear. Do talk things through or unburden yourself, even for one session, with either your GP, a leader at your place of worship, psychotherapist or a member of Cruse Bereavement Care. As many members of your family will be going through their own grieving, a professional figure is not emotionally involved and can be most helpful. This is OK and is not an indulgence.

> **Tip** Don't try to be too brave.

A widow said she has very powerful and disturbing dreams following the death of her husband. She realised that this was her body and mind adjusting while she was sleeping, and she felt she needed to understand these dreams, so she sought professional help. She said the sessions were very beneficial and enlightening.

Anger

Anger is an entirely normal part of the grieving process. You might, for example, feel angry with yourself, perhaps for not having done more for your late husband during his lifetime. You might, on the other hand, feel angry with him for leaving you in a difficult position, either emotionally or financially. It sometimes happens, also, that after her husband's death, a widow discovers some aspect of his life that she had no inkling of.

Anger is often the product of unexpressed hurt. In any case, one widow once said: 'Anger is a bit like nits. It isn't wrong to get it; it is, however, inadvisable to keep it.' She also said: 'Anger, like nits, spreads.'

> **Tip** If anger has been troubling you for longer than you feel is appropriate for you, seek professional help.

YOU ARE NOT ALONE

YOU HAVE YOURSELF

Guilt

You might feel guilty that some old issues with your other half had never been fully discussed, and that now it is too late. Most husbands or partners would wish you to make the most of the years that are left to you.

> **Tip** Forgive yourself.

House and home

Three tips, in no particular order.

Tip 1 A country-based widow said that whenever she goes back home to a dark house at the end of the day or after a holiday, she immediately turns on all the lights and makes a roaring fire in her sitting room. She finds that the lights and the fire act almost like a person, providing company and comfort. Indeed, many widows agree on the life-enhancing quality of a real fire – or even a gas fire.

Tip 2 You may want to keep all or some of your husband's clothes and belongings. There are two extremes to avoid here.

Some widows get rid of everything immediately, and then regret it. One widow moved house and got rid of all her husband's possessions within the first four months, thinking that a clean sweep would help her make a new life for herself. Later, she bitterly regretted this impulsive action.

Continued

Others, on the other hand, wish to keep everything for ever. There are many different reasons for this – the comfort of being surrounded by familiar possessions; a guilty fear that in getting rid of the husband's possessions they would also be getting rid of his memory; or worries about the empty spaces that are left by any clear-out. One widow told me she had spent far too long – eleven years – holding on to her husbands possessions and wearing black; and to this day she has never touched his study. Which leads us on to the general point, agreed on by all grief counsellors, that it is a mistake to make a shrine.

So the question arises: how many of your husband's possessions do you give away, and when? It is your choice. However, there are guidelines that most widows would agree on. In the immediate aftermath of the funeral, it is surely a good idea not to give anything of his away, rather than to distribute his possessions too hastily and then regret it.

One idea for making use of your husband's shirts and ties in a way that is both creative and comforting. Fine Cell Work is a charity that

Continued

specialises in teaching long-term prisoners how to sew often highly personalised objects that are made to order. One widow took along her husband's large collection of stripy Jermyn Street shirts and brightly coloured silk ties to be turned into patchwork quilts and cushion covers, respectively.

Tip 3 I have heard what follows again and again, and cannot emphasise its importance enough. Unless it is an absolute necessity from the financial point of view, do not sell your home in the first year of your widowhood. It is bad enough to lose your husband; but to add to this the emotional upheaval of a house move is highly inadvisable. I have heard numerous stories of widows who made this mistake and then bitterly regretted it.

Household responsibilities

Many widows find it a daunting prospect to be totally responsible, for the first time ever, for the practical intricacies of all aspects of their daily lives. One widow told me that she was sometimes quite unable to comprehend legal and financial forms and documents that had to be dealt with.

Tip Certainly for the first few months, you need to have a good trustworthy friend or relative nearby, geographically speaking, to offer essential advice and support with the endless paperwork, much of which will be quite new to you. Failing that, a solicitor or accountant will always be there; equally, they will always charge you. In any case, as one widow found, forms that have been filled out incorrectly will always bounce back at you.

The telephone can also complicate matters even more, when the person on the other end of the line uses jargon and terminology that you find incomprehensible. Sometimes they will be quite happy to repeat and explain; other times not. Try not to take it personally. In any case, you will have to learn to persevere until their meaning is clear to you.

· Tip Once more, don't be afraid to ask and ask again. It is an opportunity for people to help you, and you would help them too, in very different circumstances.

Emergencies

When you become a widow you will find yourself completely alone, perhaps for the first time, and you will sometimes feel very vulnerable. If any emergency should arise, especially in the first few months, do not hesitate to ask for help, even if that means appealing to other people's better nature.

Story: A new widow told me she had a puncture at 85 mph in the fast lane approaching the M5/M6 interchange. She managed to pull over onto the hard shoulder, and in order to get out of the car safely, she had to climb over the gearstick (not easy) and get out of the passenger door. Grabbing her handbag, she climbed over the barrier, got behind her car and phoned the breakdown services. It was dark, windy and raining, and she had no raincoat. 'I've got a puncture, I'm an OAP, and I've just been widowed,' she wailed, trying to hold back her tears. Help came very quickly!

Tip In extreme circumstances, do not hesitate to use your widowhood, even if that means becoming utterly pathetic.

Money II

If, immediately after you husband has died, you are contacted by someone claiming that he owed them money, you must refer this person (no matter how respectable they sound) to your solicitor. Widows are prime targets for people claiming money dishonestly, and it is surprising how many of them fall for this familiar scam.

A widow sent me a letter telling the following story. 'I knew that my husband always paid promptly on receipt of goods or services, and I was therefore surprised to receive a letter from a dental supplier that he had had dealings with, but through his own dentist. I contacted the dentist, who was horrified and furious, since he owed nothing.'

Tip 1 If anyone calls saying your husband owed money and asking for payment, refer that person to your solicitor. No exceptions.

Tip 2 If you have never had a solicitor, it might be advisable, after your husband's death, to choose one who suits your own circumstances, whether these be modest, average, or comfortable.

Continued

Different firms cater for different needs, and a good country-based firm, rather than one based in London or a major city, is often the answer. Their fees are frequently far lower for exactly the same service.

Practicalities

This is a practical tip that a widow told me. She sleeps
for one week on her side of her large double bed,
and then the next sleeps on her husband's side.
This seemed strange at first, but she then found it
comforting. It also saved on the laundry!

> **Tip** Use your imagination and try to be flexible.

Walking

Walking is famously therapeutic.

One widow told me that for a couple of weeks after the death of her husband she spent hours every day walking and muttering to herself (she didn't care what passers-by thought, and luckily she lived by the sea). This helped her to deal with the initial shock of losing her husband, and she would always return home physically tired, but emotionally better.

Another widow, aged fifty, whose husband had recently died, walked the entire length of Offa's Dyke with a friend of hers, completing the journey in a series of three-day sessions. The exercise; the change of scene; the beauty of the countryside; the physical challenge – all these things were immensely beneficial and helped her to look outwards towards the world, rather than inwards towards herself.

Tip 1 Go for long walks. A good hour's walk a day gets you out, and you always feel better for it.

Tip 2 Even if you don't feel like a walk, it is important to get out every day. So meet up with friends; go out for coffee or meals; anything! It all

Continued

helps you not to continually focus on your loss. It doesn't stop the grieving process, but it will temporarily distract you; and it is distraction that we need.

Tip 3 The most important muscle in your whole body is your smile.

Tip 4 Some widows say that having a pet – some animal to hold or stroke – helps enormously. Taking a dog for a walk also enables you to meet other dog owners.

Going alone

In some marriages, husbands and wives have gone to films, concerts, social evenings and on holidays together, whereas others have had independent interests and are more familiar with being by themselves socially. For many widows, going out by themselves (i.e. not with a friend) is very frightening and strange, not only logistically, in terms of travel arrangements, but also in terms of coping in a new social environment by themselves. A widow wrote that it was difficult at first, especially when she had experienced such lovely times together with her husband. She took courage and started on a long-weekend escorted tour to Berlin and found that most people can get on with other travellers for three or four days. She discovered that she had lots of things in common with her fellow travellers and she had good discussions with them, although there were moments when she missed her husband dreadfully. Since then, she has gone on other escorted local and foreign tours by herself. Now she also sometimes travels with another widow. They both say the world is their oyster.

Tip Give it a go.

Miscellaneous thoughts and maxims

What follows is a miscellaneous assortment of thoughts about widowhood that I have picked up along the way.

'Being a widow is not an illness.'

'What does "cope" mean?' This was one widow's frustrated response to the endlessly asked question about how she was coping.

'If other women can cope with widowhood, so can I.'

How do you reply to the question 'How are you?' Realising that most people do not really want to hear the details, one widow has discovered a neat solution. Her answer is invariably: 'It depends,' always said with a smile.

Someone commented to a widow that time heals. 'No it doesn't,' she said. 'But time helps you cope better.'

'The second year is the worst. That's when the reality sinks in.'

Three weeks after her husband's death, a widow, who had been happily married for many years, wrote the following sentence in a round robin to her friends. 'Don't forget that I'm always available.' The ambiguity of the statement – no doubt entirely unintended – caused numerous chuckles.

'Allow yourself to feel all the bewildering feelings. Don't suppress them; but don't indulge in them either.'

A small bouquet of tips from an aged widow: get involved in something locally; when you get up, plan your day; cook good meals for yourself and sit at a table; have the radio or television on all day for company.

A widow writing to me said that she had the greatest of difficulties in coming to terms with the death of her husband. She knew this could be achieved, but she found it so hard. She eventually found that visualising the many happy times they had spent together became a great therapy for her.

Treasure your friends.

However tempting it might be, avoid the mistake of boring your friends endlessly with your loss. They will certainly ask you how you are coping, and will be willing to listen up to a point, but no more. If, therefore, you feel the need to talk regularly and at length, it should be to a paid professional.

When – and if – you can, join a group to either learn something new, play an instrument, sport or game or discuss any topic that interests you. Try to steer away from only attending women's groups. Try a mixed group as well. A widow in her seventies said she had recently been invited to a home, along with many married couples, for a Sunday brunch. She said she loved being in this mixed company again, and hadn't realised how much she had missed men's conversations.

Accept as many invitations as you can in the first few years, and try to be a really good guest. If you continually say no to your friends' invitations to come out, they will think eventually that you are not interested or wish to be left alone.

Sometimes you will come across men who, for a fleeting moment, look just like your husband. It is very painful.

'The opposite to a dark hole is light. Seek it.'

'Today is today,' said one widow.

'KBO,' said one woman, when asked how to cope with widowhood. 'Keep buggering on', in other words.

'You will know when you need a quiet day at home.'

'Be gentle with yourself. Spoil yourself. Don't rush.'

'Going to work saved me.'

'Widowhood is not for sissies.'

A thought expressed by the journalist Felicity Green: 'I have plenty of people to do things with. I just have no one to do nothing with.'

'Who would you have thought that after three years of widowhood I miss my husband's most irritating habits. I would give anything to have him snoring next to me in bed.'

You

When widowhood arrives, some women lose their self-esteem and confidence, temporarily or even permanently. One widow told me that when she was in her twenties, looking after four very young children, she had hardly any time to brush her own hair, let alone apply makeup. Knowing that it would make her feel better, her husband used occasionally to say to her, 'Go and put your face on, darling.' Ardent feminists might not approve, but she did indeed always feel better for it, seeing her face in the mirror, tidied up and not looking so tired. She said that many years later, as a widow, it was so important to take that small amount of extra time (which she now had) to put on a little makeup. Afterwards, catching her face in the mirror, she always felt braver and better prepared to face the world.

If you can possibly afford it, give yourself regular treats – manicures, pedicures, facials, the odd massage, or even a Reiki treatment. If your relationship with your deceased husband was a tactile one – holding hands, etc. – you will now sorely miss this aspect of life, and although a beauty therapist cannot replace it, you will feel all the better, and quite possibly even a little happier, for pampering yourself.

In the immediate aftermath of her husband's death, one widow found herself overwhelmed by the sheer weight of new and unfamiliar responsibilities, and accordingly, her shoulders siezed up painfully. In this case, a few visits to the physiotherapist were not only helpful, but even essential.

Tip Take loving care of yourself.

Part IV

The years after
he dies

Consolations

You can watch any programme on the television, listen to any radio programme, see any film at the cinema, go to any play or concert any time you choose. You can eat anything, or nothing, any time you wish to. You can go to bed at any time, or stay in bed as long as you want. In short, you are an entirely free agent – even though you will often wonder whether this is a good thing. You now have the opportunity to create new ideas of how you wish to live. You can also choose to spend your money in whatever way you want, and without having to consider the needs of your spouse.

Habits

It is a good idea to try out new patterns of living that do not continually remind you of times together, which will often be too painful to be reminded of.

For example, one widow told me that Sundays had always been special for her and her husband – getting up late; reading the papers; a late breakfast. Now she gets up early on Sundays, goes for a walk by the Thames and sometimes goes to church. Then, taking with her the newspapers she hasn't had time to read during the week, she has a leisurely cooked breakfast at a local café, which always involves numerous cups of coffee. After this she walks home, generally getting back by eleven in the morning. Her Sunday routine is thus entirely different.

To further illustrate the risks involved in repeating patterns established with your deceased husband: another widow made the mistake of going to a concert very soon after her husband's death. They had regularly shared this pleasure together, but she then found herself sitting beside the only empty seat in the entire concert hall. She left in the interval.

Merry husbands

A significant number of widows have told me that they had been upset and rather shocked to receive advances from the husbands of their own girlfriends, shamelessly suggesting that they should meet up for a discreet lunch, and more. Quite clearly, the men thought that these widows now had certain needs that they – the men – were more than happy to meet. The most upsetting aspect of these advances was the undisguised opportunism of them, and the attitude they revealed.

Merry widows

A widow who starts an affair or marries again rather too soon after the death of her husband will often attract critical comments. Whatever you do, it is your life and you only live it once. Do what you wish, bearing in mind that sometimes you will attract critical comments, since in the minds of many people the old-fashioned view of how a widow should behave still dominates.

In the immediate aftermath of your husband's death, there are risks associated with entering a new relationship. You might, without thinking about it, expect the new relationship to be similar in every way to the one you had with your husband. Bear in mind, however, that some older men are most anxious to remarry, and that there is a risk that his new wife will find herself more mother-carer than spouse.

Tip 1 Take your time.

A widow touched upon another sensitive subject. If you find someone who you really want to share your life with, be aware that sometimes this can cause anxiety or much worse for either your or his children. (It is usually about money or property.) You always hope that your or his children would wish you to be happy and cared for, but this doesn't always happen.

Tip 2 Talk to your children and help them understand your wishes.

A practical approach to death

Your husband would be well advised to update the following details annually and make them known to you.

The same applies not only to your husband, but also to you, after your husband dies and before you do. In other words, you too should, as a widow, update this information annually and make it known to your next of kin, so that when you die, it will be as easy as possible for your heirs and executors to sort out your estate.

Will. Who has it? Who are the solicitors and executors? Is there a letter setting out your wishes? If there is, you should be aware that it is not a legally binding document, so you should be sure to choose executors on whom you can rely to carry out your wishes after you die.

Insurance. For travel, health, critical illness, life, buildings. You should leave a detailed list of your insurance for all these things, including names, contact details, and reference numbers for the various brokers and companies involved.

Bank and account number. While husband and wife are both alive, you should make sure that you have a joint account, since any account in the name of the deceased only will automatically be frozen the time of death. (For more details, see the Appendix, page 65.)

Shares and other investments. List details of all holdings and name(s) of your stockbroker(s) and financial advisers.

Pension. Ditto.

Safety deposit box. Location of key, and preferably give joint access to the box following your death.

Property. Write down all details concerning landlords, mortgages, letting agents, and the location of all title deeds.

Jewellery. Allocate before you die, and speak to your accountant.

Clothing and personal effects. Who should go through them and dispose of them? Make regular wardrobe clear-outs, remembering what you are leaving behind.

Papers and documents. File away and clear out regularly, so that everything is as clear and as trouble-free as possible for your heirs and executors.

Photos. It is a nice idea, for those who come after you, to go through your old photos writing down on the back who is who in them.

Children. Designate a preferred guardian.

Pets. Ditto.

Gifts. You can give away up to £3,000 a year tax-free (not £3,000 per recipient, but £3,000 in total). It is only sensible to use this allowance – whilst of course not going short yourself. (For more details, see the Appendix, page 65.)

Mementos. Who would appreciate one?

Passwords and codes on your computer. Leave a list of these together with any other helpful advice about opening files.

Arguments and rifts. Resolve if possible.

Funeral and burial or cremation. Leave clear instructions for these, as well as the funds to pay for them.

Medical history. Just in case you develop a critical disease or have an accident that leaves you incapacitated, you should write down details of your medical history, your blood group, and the name of your doctor.

Create a living will. Doctors will do everything in their power to keep you alive, even when death is imminent. If you do not wish them to prolong your life beyond its natural duration, you should consider writing a living will.

Power of attorney. Do discuss power of attorney. In the event that you as a widow are no longer capable of managing your own affairs, power of attorney to allow others to do so should be in place. You should think about this as soon as you can after becoming a widow. Do keep on asking detailed questions and explanations of your accountant and solicitor.

Lastly, put information concerning all the above in one single, secure place, and tell your solicitor or trusted confidant where it is. Do not, in other words, divulge this information before you die.

Appendix

Gifts

A competent accountant informs me that at the time of writing (2013) the annual exemption for gifts which will not be acculmulated with the estate at death is £3,000. In plain English, this means that you can give away a total of £3,000 every year with no tax implications. If you do not use this exemption, it can be carried forward one year.

There are also permitted unlimited gifts. One can give away separate sums of £250 to any number of individuals in one year. In theory, therefore, the entire estate could be disposed of with no Inheritance Tax being due; this provided that no one recipient received more than £250 in any one year. Note, too, that the £250 cannot be added to the £3,000 tax-exempt gift so as to give one person a total of £3,250. The rule is £250 per recipient.

Furthermore, where an individual has excess income over their normal expenditure as required to maintain their usual standard of living, that individual is allowed to give away all or any part of that excess without its being regarded as a gift for the purposes of Inheritance Tax. However, such gifts have to be 'normal' for the donor. In other words, a miser (for example) would not be able to demonstrate that exceptional acts of generosity should be tax-exempt.

Lastly, the annual £3,000 and the gifts out of income can be made to individuals and/or organisations; whereas the £250 gifts must be to individuals.

Joint bank accounts

A competent accountant writes:

'I agree absolutely that the general expenditure account should be a joint account.

'What is also appropriate is for the widow or widower to immediately bring in another member of the family into a joint account, so that it will remain operational if the widow or widower were to become incapacitated.

'Unless you choose and declare otherwise, the value of that account will be regarded by HMRC as 50 per cent the widow's and 50 per cent the nominated family member's, but if the account is only receiving income and paying out living expenses, that should not be an issue.

'It is possible for the nominated family member to be no more than an authorised signatory; whereas a joint bank account in the names of husband and wife will only ever be regarded as owned fifty–fifty.'

Your accountant

As previously stated, it cannot be emphasised enough that it is inadvisable in the extreme to change your accountant shortly after your spouse dies. Furthermore, where the accountant has been the adviser and financial confidant of either spouse, there is a professional duty to assist the surviving spouse and family members with regard to their affairs.

As regards understanding the financial affairs of the deceased, you should not allow yourself to be intimidated by the complexities. Any professional or expert should be able to explain, in simple English, the effects of any situation of which they are supposed to have detailed knowledge.

Acknowledgements

This book could not have been written without the tips from many widows. I am deeply grateful to them.

Amber	Liz
Angie x 2	Marcia
Anne	Marijke
Annie	Mary x 4
Caroline	Moira
Celia	Philippa
Celine	Primrose
Elizabeth	Rachel
Gillian	Rosey
Joy	Rosie
Julia	Sara
Laila	Shirley
Linda	

My thanks to Sebastian Cresswell-Turner, as I type with one finger only, and he doesn't. He also made numerous useful editorial suggestions, without which this book would not have come into existence.

Thank you to Anand and Sangeeta Shenoy and Kim Whyte for help in typesetting the book.

Further thanks to Caroline Stanley for invaluable advice on the adminstrative practicalities of death; also to Gill Kind and Alan Ford for fact-checking and advising about grief and money matters.

Poems

Remember Me

You can close your eyes and pray that he will come back,
Or you can open your eyes and see all that he has left.

Your heart can be empty as you can't see him,
Or you can be full of the love that you shared.

You can turn your back on tomorrow and live yesterday,
Or you can be happy for tomorrow because of yesterday.

You can remember him and only that he has gone,
Or you can cherish his memory and let it live on.

You can cry and close your mind, be empty and turn
your back,
Or you can do what he would want: smile, open your
eyes, love, and go on.

You can shed tears that he has gone,
Or you can smile because he lived.

David Harkins

Ode: Intimations of Immortality

What though the radiance which was once so bright
Be now for ever taken from my sight,
Though nothing can bring back the hour
Of splendour in the grass, of glory in the flower,
We will grieve not, rather find
Strength in what remains behind.

William Wordsworth

For your notes

A note on the author

Jan Robinson began collecting advice from widows after her husband died. Six months later, she decided to turn the tips into a book and sell it through her website. She has four children and lives in London.

www.tipsfromwidows.co.uk